WEATHER WORDS

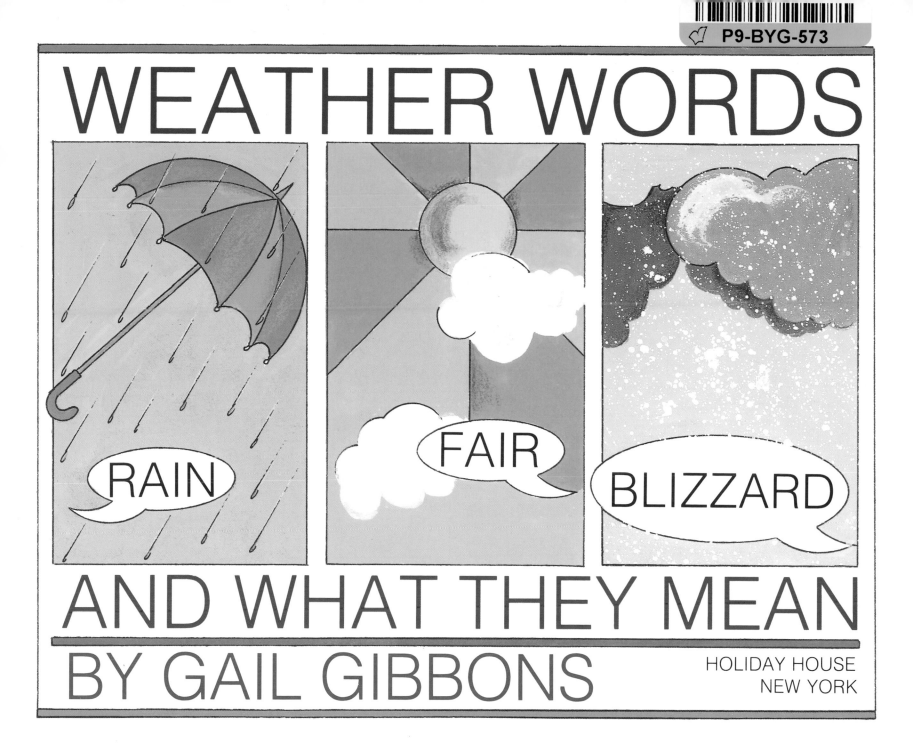

RAIN

FAIR

BLIZZARD

AND WHAT THEY MEAN

BY GAIL GIBBONS

HOLIDAY HOUSE
NEW YORK

For John Briggs

Special thanks to the
National Weather Service in
Burlington, Vermont

Copyright © 1990 by Gail Gibbons
All rights reserved
Printed & Bound in March 2015 at Tien Wah Press, Johor Bahru, Johor, Malaysia
18
Library of Congress Cataloging-in-Publication Data

Gibbons, Gail.
Weather words and what they mean / by Gail Gibbons.
p.   cm.
Summary: Introduces basic weather terms and concepts.
ISBN 0-8234-0805-1
1. Weather—Terminology—Juvenile literature.
2. Meteorology—Terminology—Juvenile literature.
[1. Weather—Terminology.
2. Meteorology—Terminology.]
I. Title.   QC981.3.G53   1990
551.6'014—dc20   89-39515   CIP   AC
ISBN 0-8234-0805-1
ISBN 0-8234-0952-X (pbk.)

ISBN-13: 978-0-8234-0805-4 (hardcover)
ISBN-13: 978-0-8234-0952-5 (paperback)

The weather changes from day to day. Weather words explain what the weather is like outside.

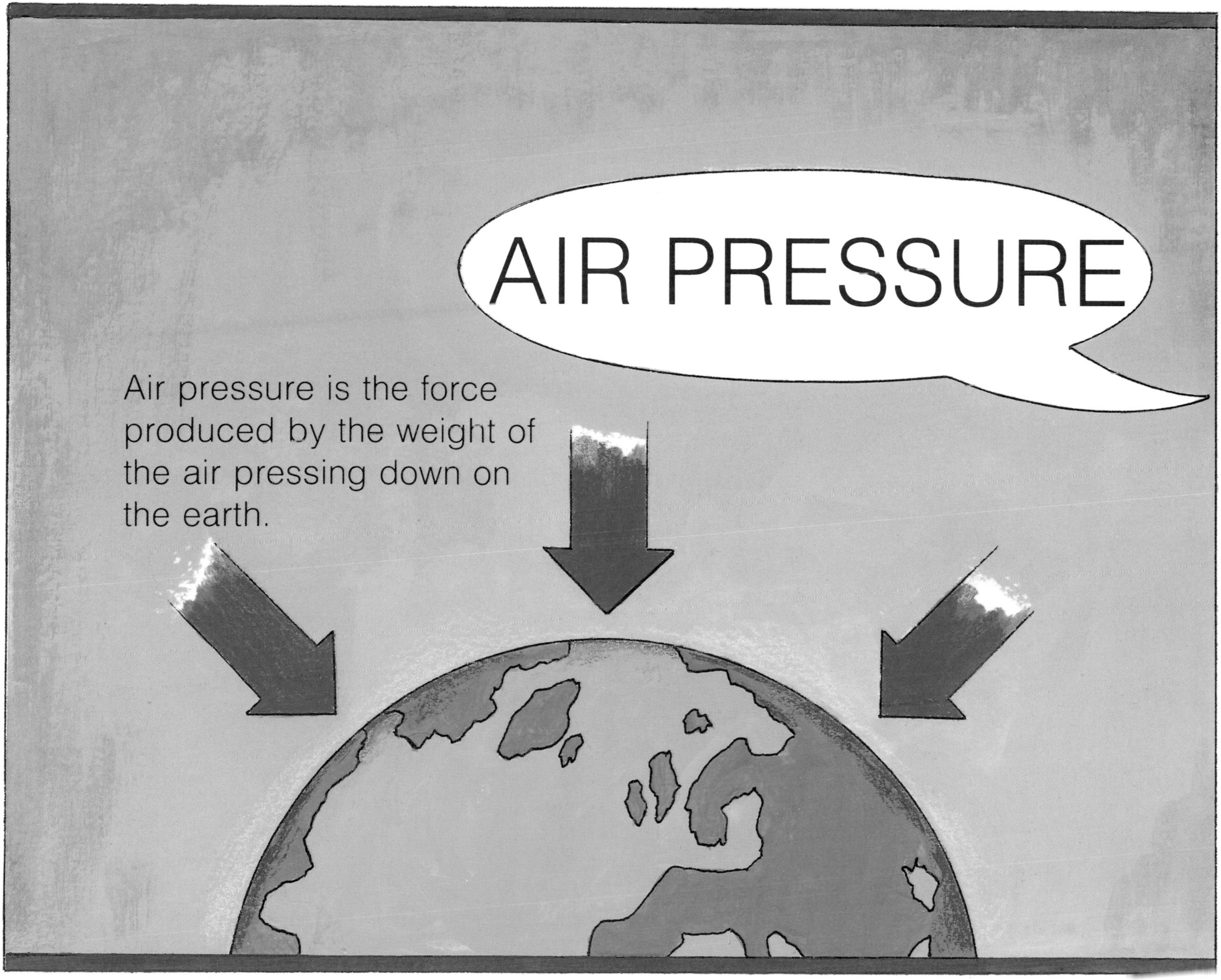
AIR PRESSURE
Air pressure is the force produced by the weight of the air pressing down on the earth.

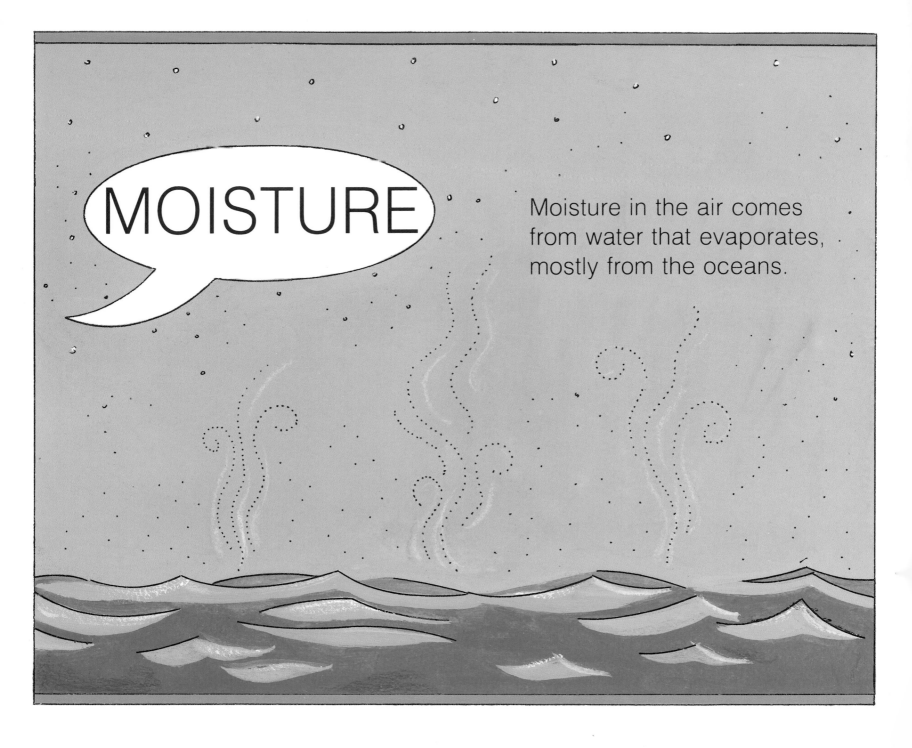

TEMPERATURE

The temperature goes up and down. When the sun rises in the morning, the air becomes warmer and the temperature goes up.

MILD

When the sun sets, the air becomes cooler and the temperature goes down.

CHILLY

The temperature also changes with the seasons. In the summer, the sun is high in the sky. The days are warm and longer.

In the winter, the sun is low in the sky. The days are cold and shorter.

AIR PRESSURE

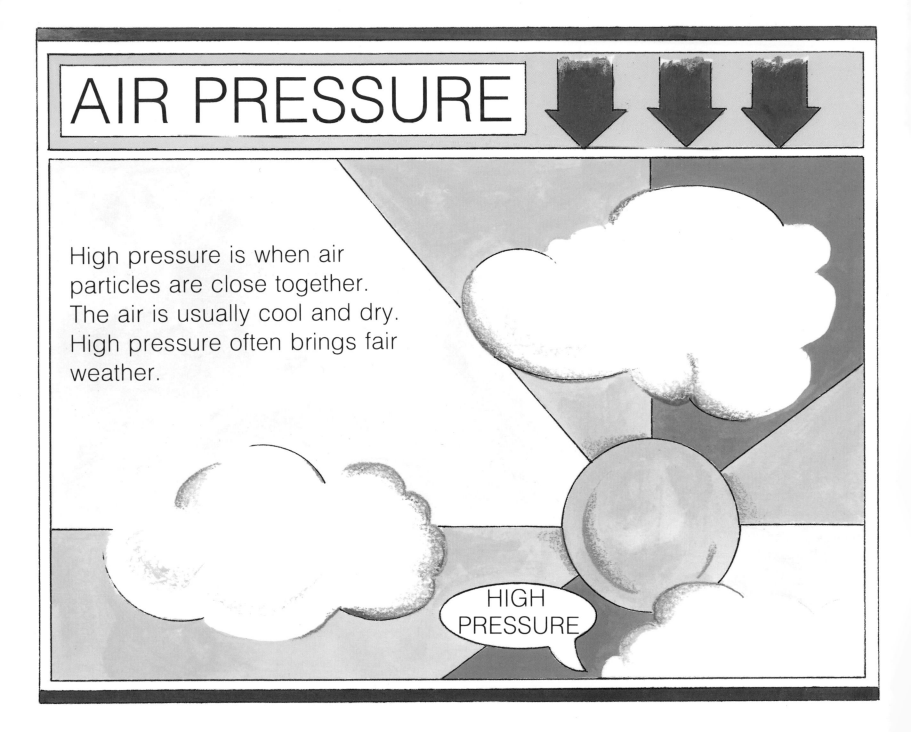

High pressure is when air particles are close together. The air is usually cool and dry. High pressure often brings fair weather.

LOW PRESSURE

Low pressure is when the air particles are farther apart. The air is usually warm and moist. Low pressure often brings bad weather.

water vapor
or ice crystals

Moisture makes clouds, too.
When water evaporates from
rivers, lakes and oceans, it is
called vapor. It moves up with
the warm air and forms little
drops of water or ice crystals.
A cloud is formed.

warm air

Clouds come in all shapes and sizes. There are three main kinds of clouds.

Cumulus clouds are puffy. They are fair weather clouds.

PARTLY SUNNY

PARTLY CLOUDY

Cirrus clouds are the highest clouds. They mean fair weather, too.

CLOUDY

Stratus clouds are low, gray clouds. Sometimes, they bring rain or snow.

There are other kinds of clouds with long names. They are combinations of cumulus, cirrus and stratus clouds.

Cirrocumulus clouds usually mean changing weather.

Cirrostratus clouds often bring rain or snow.

Nimbostratus clouds bring rain or snow.

A cloud close to the earth's surface is called fog.

When enough electricity builds up, it bursts through the cloud and flashes. This is called lightning. Lightning is very hot. It heats the air around it. The hot air expands and . . . BOOM! It makes a loud noise called thunder.

RAINBOW

Everyone loves looking at a rainbow! This may happen while it is raining, or just after the rain stops. When sunbeams shine through drops of rain, the light breaks up into seven colors. A rainbow appears.

Sometimes in the winter it snows. Snow crystals form when water freezes inside the clouds.

When the snow crystals join together, they become snowflakes.

When they are heavy enough, they fall.

Snow falls to the earth in different ways.

FLURRIES

Flurries are when it snows lightly.

SNOWSTORM

A snowstorm is when a lot of snow falls. It can be windy.

Sleet is snow that melts and refreezes before it hits the ground.

SLEET

SNOW

A normal snowfall occurs when there is little or no wind.

BLIZZARD

A blizzard is a very heavy snowstorm. The snow becomes deeper and deeper and the wind howls.

Sometimes it hails. Inside the cloud ice crystals are tossed up and down. Water vapor freezes onto the ice crystals in layers. When they become heavy enough, they fall as hailstones.

WIND

Wind happens when warm air moves up and cooler air moves in to replace it. Warm and cool temperatures affect the wind speed and direction. Wind direction is where the wind comes from.

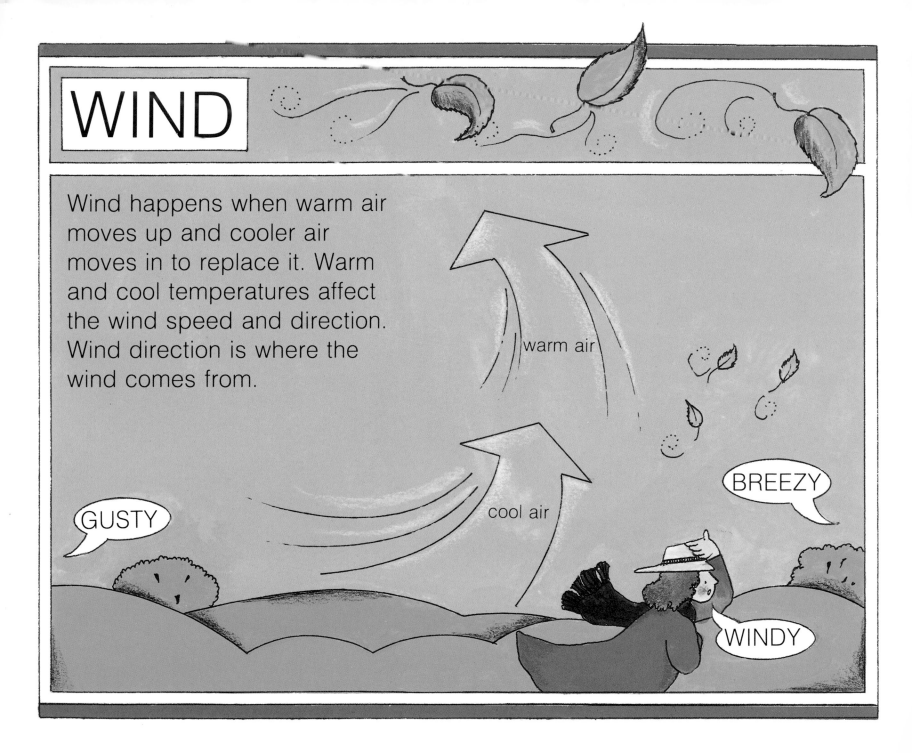

When wind blows with more and more force, a windstorm develops. There are many kinds of windstorms. Often, they cause damage.

A hurricane is a spiral-shaped windstorm that comes from the tropics.

HURRICANE

A gale is a strong windstorm.

GALE

A tornado is a funnel-shaped windstorm that twists as hot air spins upward.

TORNADO

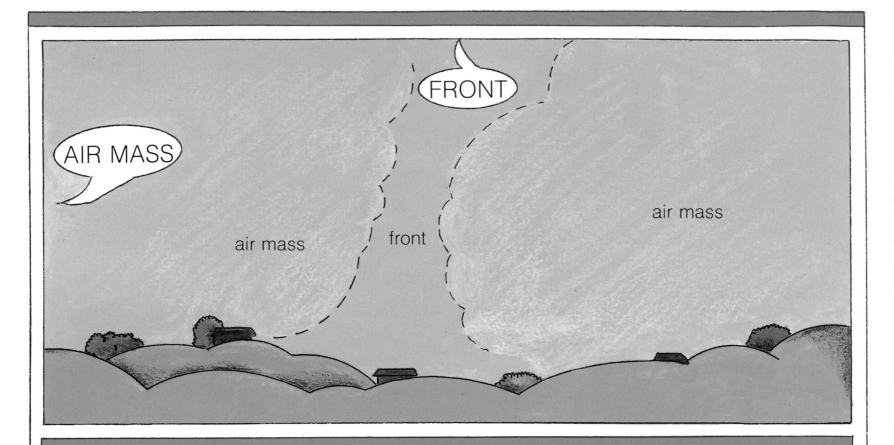

The many combinations of temperature, air pressure, moisture and wind create different kinds of weather conditions. A big area of weather that is the same is called an air mass. The boundary between two air masses is called a front. This boundary is where the weather changes.

The weather is hardly ever the same from day to day.
That's why it is so interesting.

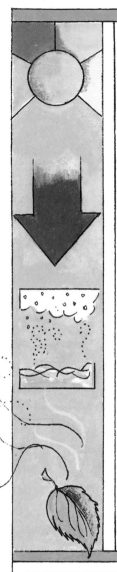

The driest place in the world is a desert in Chile. It hasn't rained there for over 400 years.

A number of years ago in France, a tornado crossed a pond and sucked up everything. At the place where the tornado stopped, the people had a surprise rainfall of fish and frogs!

There is enough electricity in one flash of lightning to light a house for one year.

It rains more days each year on Kauai, Hawaii than in any other place in the world. There it rains about 350 days a year.

The coldest recorded temperature was in Antarctica. It was −126° Fahrenheit (−88° Centigrade).

The hottest recorded temperature was in Northern Africa. It was 136° Fahrenheit (58° Centigrade).

Sound travels at 1088 feet per second. If you are one mile from lightning, it will take about five seconds for the sound of thunder to reach you.

It's believed that no two snowflakes are ever the same.

The highest wind speed ever *recorded* was 231 miles per hour in 1934 on Mt. Washington in New Hampshire.

REMEMBER . . .
When you hear a weather forecast that gives storm warnings, pay attention. Be careful.